INDIAN CARPETS

A HAND-KNOTTED HERITAGE

INDIAN CARPETS

A HAND-KNOTTED HERITAGE

AshaRani Mathur

Rupa & Co

Text & Pictures Copyright © AshaRani Mathur 2004

Published 2004 by

Rupa • Co

7/16, Ansari Road, Daryaganj
New Delhi 110 002

Sales Centres:
Allahabad Bangalore Chandigarh Chennai
Hyderabad Jaipur Kathmandu
Kolkata Ludhiana Mumbai Pune

Book Design & Typeset by
Arrt Creations
45 Nehru Apts Kalkaji, New Delhi 110 019

Printed in India by
Ajanta Offset & Packagings Ltd

Pg 1: Detail from Jaipur Mughal carpet, Kashmir.
Pg 2: Detail from Modi Kashan carpet, Kashmir.
Pg 3: Detail from mid-17th century Mughal carpet, Lahore.
Pg 5: Border of Kassan carpet, Jaipur.

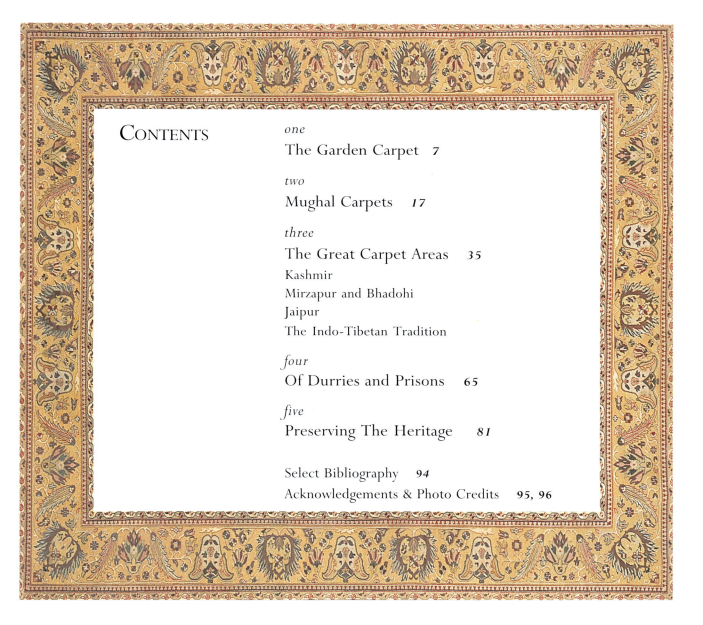

CONTENTS

THE GARDEN CARPET

*W*hen we look at an old carpet, a hundred stories come to life, shimmering from its motifs in jewelled colours, from its worn pile, its subtle weaves. Stories of who made it, and how; of the matchless skills that went into its making, and its countless months and years on the loom. Beyond those first perceptions, there are the questions of why it was made and for whom; the legends it depicts and their meaning; and the saga of its passage through the centuries: in all these lie the very breath of romance.

This book, then, begins with a single old carpet: the Garden Carpet of Jaipur: a carpet of such vast dimensions that its length stretches

opp. Close up of a garden plot. The amazing detailing includes delicate outlining of animals, leaves and birds' feathers.

almost the width of a museum hall. It was not made in India; it was woven in Persia, perhaps in Kirman, perhaps near Isfahan; but no matter, for in it we see the source of the tradition that was brought to this country by the Mughals and brilliantly adopted by Indian weavers. This carpet is also a very old one: records indicate it came to Jaipur in 1632, during the reign of Mirza Raja Jaisinghji I. It is, in fact, the oldest known Garden Carpet in the world to survive intact, and one of the finest examples of this genre. If we accept that it could have taken over two decades to weave — so detailed and intricate is its patterning — then it dates back to the early 17th century, perhaps even the late 16th century, and was almost certainly begun during the reign of the great Shah Abbas of Persia. Without question its temperament, its appearance, belong to an imperial era and reflect all the rich images of such a time.

Beyond its age and size, however, it is the theme of the carpet and the fantasies it evokes that are so compelling. In the centre, a majestic blue-domed pavilion surmounts a central

Central pool and pavilion, its blue dome surmounted by Chinese cloud bands, seen laterally. From this angle we can see the mirror-image nature of the carpet's construction, also the preying of animals one on the other.

tank. The pavilion is decorated for the pleasure of an emperor; from its splendid throne he could gaze upon, and enjoy, the profusion of the natural and animal life displayed around him in such vibrant detail. The entire ground is divided into four, the Char Bagh or four-fold garden of Islamic metaphor. Yet this may be simply a realistic representation of Shah Abbas's own city of Isfahan where he caused channels to be cut from the river Zind-e-ruh ("the river of life"). His own pavilion, the Hasht Behist, the eight-fold paradise, overlooked extensive gardens with avenues of trees and water canals with sparkling fountains. But the unsung artist who designed the Jaipur carpet added elements of fantasy to create a world that is at once life-like and filled with mythical figures.

An abundance of water runs through the carpet: first, the major channels which divide the ground into four, and then all the little streams, pools and tanks that seem to exist only to create the sub-divisions that allow the designer scope to express his dreams of the real and the unreal. In the vivid detailing there are areas where the formality of a garden gives way to the tumult of an imagined forest, scene of the animals and birds of fable, supernatural in shape and intent.

In all there are fifty two parts arranged in the four quadrangles around the central tank, the basic designs being thirteen which are repeated in different colours across the carpet. But this bare-bones description does no justice to its sheer vitality nor to the riot of images and colours that delight the viewer. The water channels teem with fish, and duck with their

opp. Close up of the pavilion at the centre of the carpet; the burnt bricks of the building look so realistic, they appear to be painted rather than woven.

wings spread back as if in motion, an effect enhanced by the ripples and eddies in the water. There is an exuberance of vegetation, flowering bushes and stately trees like the cypress and varieties of plane, or fruit trees laden with peaches, apples, dates and pomegranates. Their broad, spreading branches give shelter to perched and nested birds of all kinds, pheasants, parrots, cranes and some which are small and exotically beautiful. The lushness and profusion indicate a garden in spring, a youthfulness on the verge of summer ripeness.

But all is not idyllic in this garden. As hard, as gritty, as the baked brick walls of the pavilion are the scenes of ferocity where animals mythical and real attack and prey upon one another. The keylin, the unicorn of Chinese legend, appears with the bodies of a lion and a stag, the one held in the iron jaws of the other; a dragon devours a fish; and in a chain of violence, a pheasant assaults a duck which in turn grabs a fish's tail in its beak. Nor are the birds left behind: they swoop eagerly towards their prey. Such combats were commonly depicted in other carpets of this genre and serve as an allegory for the battle between good and evil, an Islamic convention.

above & opp:
We can see how the different garden plots are laid out along the water course. Each has its own vitality where the flowering trees and plants nourish and shelter a variety of animal and bird life.

The magnitude of activity on the carpet, spread over its length and breadth, leads us to an admiration for the weavers whose nimble fingers brought it to life. From the width of the carpet, just over twelve feet, we may imagine that at least four to six weavers must have sat shoulder to shoulder on the loom to work on it. And its length, a full twenty eight feet, indicates it must have taken long to complete; such a complex work certainly would have meant years of hard labour. To which we should add the time taken to weave in all the special effects of light and shade by using subtly different colours, the rich red of the ground providing the base for chromatic variations in greens, blues, yellows, pinks, browns and greys. The deep blue border depicts a creeper which joins its floral motifs of palmettes, rosettes and five-petalled blossoms.

In its totality, the carpet represents the most glorious phase of the Persian tradition which achieved its height in the reign of Shah Abbas. A scholar has written: "In the 16th century Persian craftsmen carried carpet-weaving to heights never attained before or since, producing with miraculous skill designs unparalleled in beauty."

It was this tradition that travelled to India to create an enduring industry here.

opp. Close up of a plot at the carpet's corner. Held within the scrolled floral outer borders,
a number of birds cluster in, around, under flowering trees.

t w o

MUGHAL CARPETS

*E*ven before the arrival of the Persian Garden Carpet in Jaipur, hand-knotted carpets had been woven in India. The tradition of floor coverings is an ancient one in this country, but our particular reference at this point is to pile carpets, whose techniques originated with the nomadic peoples of Turkey, the Caucasus and Central Asia. As with all people on the move, they used materials that were readily available: wool, for the most part, easy to obtain from their own herds of sheep and goats. Their horizontal looms were simple and portable; on them, they wove carpets that they could use not only as floor coverings but also as blankets and screens, as saddle covers or bags to wrap their goods. Their basic

opp. This 19th c. carpet is a copy of the 17th c Mughal style, with the conventional palmettes, birds and cloud bands. The cartouches on the border also depict birds.

techniques were refined in the great courts of medieval Islam, like those at Samarqand and Isfahan, from where they travelled to India. But when exactly the tradition took root here is open to question. We know that the 16th century ruler of Kashmir, Zain-ul-Abidin, brought in carpet weavers from Central Asia. He it was who made Kashmir into a "garden of crafts"; but after his reign, much of what he had established was swept away in the turbulence of the times that followed.

As always, the longest-lasting impetus came from the Mughals. The early history of the dynasty deeply influenced them towards Persian aesthetics, and without doubt the courts of monarchs like Shah Abbas represented a high point of refinement and culture that the Mughals both

keenly appreciated and emulated. It was Emperor Akbar, indefatigable pursuer of beautiful objects, who set up the first recorded workshops or karkhanas for pile carpets. He brought in skilled weavers from Persia so that the art could be taught to local craftsmen and sustained by them. The rest, as they say, is history.

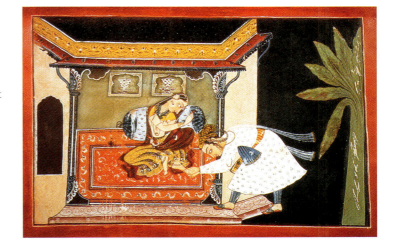

Well before Akbar's time carpets were regarded not just as decorations, but also symbols of power and wealth. An entire department, the Farrashkhana, was traditionally placed in charge of the storage and maintenance of textiles of courtly splendour such as carpets, awnings, screens and tents, and a small army of officials and retainers kept them in readiness for use. The

The Offended Mistress, Pahari painting, last quarter of 17th c. The lady is clearly disgusted with her errant lover; but the way she is seated on the carpet with a bolster illustrates how carpets were used as floor coverings for people to sit on.

opp. Saroukh Turkoman carpet, Kashmir, wool, reproduction of an antique Central Asian tribal carpet. Originally this would have been used as a door hanging.

ruler was, of necessity, quite often on the move, to go into battle, to inspect his far-flung domains, or to form alliances. A monarch on the march was an impressive sight; all the accoutrements of luxury were carried on elephant back to be set up in the vast encampments that marked the stages of a journey. Poor indeed was the king who could not dazzle the local population — and, by inference, his enemies — or outshine his allies with an opulent display of gold-threaded tents, tapestried awnings and rich and costly carpets.

No dynasty realised the effect of a show of pomp more than the Mughals, masters of the art of public magnificence. Carpets decorated their courts in many ways: spread on the floor for people to sit or stand on, or hung on walls and niches as screens, the finest woven as prayer mats.

In Akbar's reign meticulous records were kept of the contents of the Farrashkhana stores, which included the number of carpets held and their origin. We know from the writings of Abul Fazl in the Ain-i-Akbari that the Emperor established workshops for carpets in Lahore, Agra and Fatehpur Sikri, where weaving had commenced at least by the

1580s . The progress of the workshops was rapid and the ensuing results most satisfactory; Abul Fazl was able to record: "His Majesty has caused carpets to be made of wonderful varieties and charming texture; he has appointed experienced workmen who have produced many masterpieces. The gilims of Iran (Persia) and Turan are no more thought of, although merchants still import carpets from Goshkhan, Khuzistan, Kirman and Sabzwar. All kinds of carpet weavers have settled here and drive a flourishing trade".

Detail from pg 16 shows a palmette with pheasants about it.

opp. Detail from pg 22 showing a multi-petalled palmette with a lion face inside.

Hunting animals, stylised flowers, the mythical phoenix, all derivative of the early Mughal style. But this carpet was woven in Jaipur jail in the late 19th c.

It is clear from this account that carpets from Persia were still coming into India; what is more, they were a strong influence on the local production for both technique and design. Certain Persian carpets were copied almost in totality by Indian weavers, but the inspirations for some designs came from other sources. This was one

of the great eras of miniature painting, of illuminated folios, of books whose page margins were traced with painted scrolling vines. It was also a time of superb textiles, for which India had been renowned for centuries. Gossamer fabrics were printed, brocaded or embroidered with delicate patterns repeated in rows across the body. Akbar's court hummed with activity; there were ateliers for painters and book artists, and workshops for fine textiles. It is easy to imagine that there must have been a kind of creative cross-flow, a free borrowing of ideas and motifs; indeed, scholars have surmised that some carpet designs might well have been the work of miniaturists, or at the very least influenced by them. In turn, the weavers brought an almost painterly eye to their art, knotting dyed yarns of enormous colour range and juxtaposing knots of different colours so closely as to create the effect of yet another colour.

It was not long before the art of carpet weaving reached heights of excellence, so much so that a scholar of Islamic art, Daniel Walker, has written: "…the most technically accomplished classical carpets of all time were woven in India". To better understand this remark, however, we should interrupt this brief historical overview to look at the technique of hand-knotted pile carpets. Little has changed in the basic technique, and in the present looms we see their precursors of three, four hundred years ago.

On vertical roller looms the weavers set to work on the warp (usually sturdy cotton yarn) stretched tightly top to bottom, to create, inch by inch, magic patterns in florals, geometrics and other designs. The warp runs the length of the carpet and its tension must be evenly maintained; the closer the warp threads, the finer the weave. Across this, to the

Birds Kirman, Kashmir, single-knotted, silk on silk, 360 knots per sq.in. Birds were a favourite theme of carpet artists of Mughal India, as also their patrons. Luxury fibres like silk enabled very fine knotting and an effect of colour shading.

width of the carpet, run the weft threads which pass over and under the warp; and both warp and weft provide the foundation for the rows of wool or silk knots that are tied on to form the pile, the upright yarn that will be trimmed at the end of the operation. The design of the carpet comes from the pile, so we may imagine the foundation as a giant canvas on which the pile is like a "painting" that has been knotted in. Knots in coloured yarns are tied around consecutive warp threads, and there are different sorts of knots, of which the most commonly used in India is the senneh or Persian knot. Here, the weaver ties the strand of yarn around two adjacent warp threads, circling only one warp thread while passing behind the

left: In the Mirzapur-Bhadohi area, master artist Shamsher Ali creates a design with a colour plate, an art he learned from his father. This will be transferred to graph paper as the naksha for the weaver to follow.

right: Yarn dyeing in vats, Mirzapur-Bhadohi. This is the traditional method; in this factory, used only for small lots, as the bulk is done by machine.

opp. Mughal flower carpet, ca. mid-17th c., Lahore. The flowering plants are rendered in the naturalistic style favoured at that time, as seen in the detail above.

other. In this way, the two ends of the yarn appear separately at different places: the first between the two adjacent warp threads mentioned, and the second between one of these and the next warp thread. Each knot is separated from its neighbour by a loop that is cut after the next weft is passed; each row of knots is secured in place by the passing of one or more rows of weft which are tamped or hammered down. Once the knotting has started, the wefts have to be skilfully passed so that the warp maintains its tautness and closeness of threads, and to keep the edges straight.

Working thus with coloured yarns for knotting and (usually) cotton yarns for the weft, with rows of knots interspersed with wefts, the weaver completes the carpet from side to side. Overlapping wefts are used if more than one weaver is working on the carpet. The denseness of knotting serves as an indicator of the carpet's fineness of weave; the more knots there are to the square inch, the finer it is deemed to be; and the count varies, usually from sixteen to five hundred though, exceptionally, it can go as high as one thousand. The warp threads form the fringes of the carpet and may be twisted or braided for decorative effect.

Well before the process of knotting, though, several critical stages of preparation will have already taken place, including the dyeing of the

The Abhisarika, Pahari painting, third quarter of 17th c. Night and the dark clouds provide a perfect backdrop for the sumptuous pavilion for lovers seated upon a richly-coloured carpet with a broad floral border.

opp. Flowering shrub carpet fragment, Mughal, Lahore, ca. mid-17th c.

coloured wool or silk that forms the pile. Clearly it is the design that determines how and where the knots are to be tied; it begins with the colour plate, or naksha, painted by a skilled artist, that details the patterning. Such plates could be old, as in the case of an existing design, or freshly painted when a new one is created. This serves as the master plan for the next step, which is to interpret the design in a manner that the weaver can follow, done by transferring it onto a giant sheet of graph paper where each square represents a knot and each colour a specific shade of yarn.

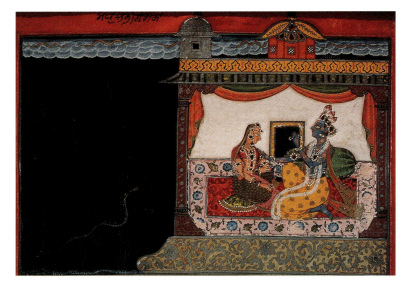

After it comes off the loom, the carpet goes through various stages of finishing, one of the most important of which is washing. This not only removes accumulated dust or dirt, but also gives the pile a lustrous sheen; special washes impart different looks to the carpet, such as muting its colours or giving it an antique patina. The excess pile has to be clipped to flatten the surface and bring out the design, further clarified through sorting, which separates the strands of

yarns so that the motifs and colours stand out. From start to finish, then, several highly skilled functions are involved.

Given the timeless appeal of carpets, the continuity of tradition and design, we can imagine that this art would have flourished in much the same manner in the great Mughal workshops of four centuries ago. Persian designs were adapted by Indian imagination, whose florals and animal representations were more fluid, more naturalistic, than the originals. But it was not until the reign of Jehangir, Akbar's son, in the 17th century that the style we call Indian truly came into its own. In that era of refinement and elegance, the prevailing taste for luxury found its way into carpets. Where once sheep's wool had formed the pile on cotton, Jehangir's weavers knotted the finest pashmina wool on a foundation of silk, the materials enabling a higher density of knots with counts of up to two thousand per square inch. In turn, this fineness allowed the expression of ever more graceful curves in the patterns; more, it permitted the subtlest of colour gradations which added depth and dimension to the design. This effect was enhanced by the nuanced shading achieved by "ton-sur-ton" or tone on tone, a coloristic device where variations of the same or

similar colours were juxtaposed without the use of hard separating outlines. These pashmina carpets, possibly the finest carpets ever made in India if not the world, are now mostly in international collections, many in fragments. The only known example in India is in the City Palace Museum in Jaipur.

We have seen that the earliest designs mostly followed the favourite themes of Persian weavers with their profusions of scrolling vines with palmettes and florals, animals both realistic and grotesque, and trees with birds. By the time Jehangir's son, Shah Jehan, came to the throne, a new style

Jaipur Mughal, Kashmir, single-knotted, wool, 324 knots per sq.in. Reproduced from an antique Jaipur Mughal design, the field encloses flowers within a trellis-like effect of lines and curves.

was apparent, that of naturalistic flowering plants set in rows. This flower style, so beloved of the Mughals, was to be seen everywhere: on shawls, textiles, jade and glass. Doubtless some of the credit for this goes to Mansur, Jehangir's celebrated court painter, whose pictures of flowers and plants have a freshness and seem to breathe life even when we look at them today. The typical Mughal carpet of this era has rows of plants in full bloom set against a vivid red ground. Later, both flower and plant became more stylised, less naturalistic, and were set within elaborate lattices often composed of curving vines. Sometimes flowers were scattered all over the ground of the carpet in clusters of tiny blooms, the so-called mille-fleur design.

Among the most intriguing carpets are those that have different shapes, round, arched, or formed like giant pennants. There are examples of these in the Jaipur museums, and it is speculated that they were especially woven for the Jaipur Raja's fort at Amer. So unusual are some of these shapes that no one knows how and where they were meant to be placed and used, though likely some were made for a tent complex.

Aurangzeb, the last great Emperor of the Mughal dynasty, did not share the aesthetic interests of his forebears. Carpets were still woven, but the artistic and lively patronage of his father and grandfather was missing. As with painting, as with many other arts, the scene shifted to regional courts where local rajas encouraged weavers to set up looms and offered the shelter of patronage.

Detail of a circular carpet tentatively ascribed to 1620-1630. The white ground, ornamented with florals and palmettes, has a central medallion.

opp. Detail of a shaped carpet, Mughal, ca. mid-17th c. Such carpets were commissioned, it is thought, for use in hunting tents.

three

THE GREAT CARPET AREAS

The decline of the Mughals and the subsequent lack of a munificent and informed patronage dispersed the art of weaving to regional courts, but there is scarce information about what happened between the 17th and the 19th centuries; certainly, there was some production, but surviving examples are few and far between. It was not until the 19th century that carpet industry in India was really revived, and the impetus came from the Great Exhibition of 1851 held at the Crystal Palace in London. Indian pile carpets, from Mirzapur and Kashmir amongst other places, were displayed to an admiring public and aroused great interest. They also attracted the attention of Western merchants, who looked beyond

opp. Kirman Laver Rahadaar, Kashmir, single-knotted, wool on wool, 431 knots per sq.in. The large medallion, with its stylised floral sprays, dominates, but does not overwhelm, the field with its delicate foliage so reminiscent of shawls.

the elegant designs, fine workmanship and rich colours to realise their commercial possibilities. Soon the first companies established themselves in Srinagar, Amritsar and Mirzapur and it was not long before the revival took place in other areas as well.

Those latter-day pioneers have been criticised for diluting the beauty of the original designs, and for introducing their own designs to be woven in India. Names like Aubusson and Savonnerie became part of the weaver's vocabulary. The colour palette changed, too, the more so after aniline dyes were brought in to speed the process of manufacture; often they were harsh and lacked the subtlety and warmth of the traditional vegetable colours. Nonetheless, the fact remains that a new life was given to the art and the foundation set for the carpet industry as we know it today.

Mirzapur-Bhadohi: a weaver operates a tufting gun on a carpet. Hand-tufted carpets are becoming popular as they are quicker to make and are priced lower than those that are hand-knotted.

below: Washing the carpet, Mirzapur-Bhadohi. This has to be done with great care as an excess or paucity of the chemicals used could damage the colour and fabric.

opp. Mirzapur-Bhadohi, a weaver works at his loom in the village of Khetalpur Khamaria.

Though we call it an industry and speak of factories and manufacture, the organisation is nothing like a "factory" as we understand the term, an industrial plant where hundreds of units are churned out every day. Handmade pile carpets are an art and a craft which need huge amounts of time and labour, and the fact is that carpet making remains a cottage industry with looms dispersed over wide rural and semi-rural areas. Yes, there are premises where a number

of looms operate together in conditions like a factory, much as the karkhanas or workshops of royal patrons used to, but the bulk of the weaving takes place in loom sheds in village homes, where weavers — often members of a family — work to order on designs and specifications provided by the exporter or carpet company. The factory is essentially the company's collection point for this production and provides the professional management required for the business end. It is the place where inventories are controlled and stocks maintained; it is the vital store-house of design and the source of raw materials such as dyed yarns as also the nakshas or designs that have to be sent to the weavers; it is where quality checks and finishing processes like clipping and sorting are carried out. From start to finish, the entire process is labour-intensive and involves specialist functions such as dyeing the yarn and washing the carpet, which may be done in the factory or (quite often) given out to a trusted contractor. Large companies with reputations to maintain are particular about each aspect of the operation, from ensuring the precise shade of yarn to monitoring the progress on the loom.

MIRZAPUR AND BHADOHI

The great carpet belt cuts a wide swathe across the mountains, deserts and plains of Northern India, from Kashmir, Ladakh and Rajasthan in the west to Arunachal Pradesh in the east. At the heart of this belt lies the Indo-Gangetic plain, the area where the largest number of looms is concentrated. The centre is formed by the districts of Mirzapur and Bhadohi in Uttar Pradesh; and its hinterland extends, however patchily, in every direction: north into the terai, east into Bihar, south into Madhya Pradesh and north-west almost till

Lucknow. Within this area is produced the widest variety of floor coverings in the country, from fine hand-knotted pile carpets to durries and gabbehs to industrial flooring made of compressed synthetics. These could be made on factory shop floors along a highway, as in the last case, or in a small loom shed in a remote village.

Hunting Tabriz, Mirzapur-Bhadohi, wool, 414 knots per sq.in. The spectacular central medallion with a flower-burst at its heart is set within a field of leaves and vines where animals prey on each other, an old Mughal theme.

But the most intense activity is around Mirzapur and Bhadohi, situated on either side of the river Ganga as she flows eastward from Allahabad to Varanasi. If we take the highway between the two cities as an axis, then the looms are sited to a depth of fifty kilometres on either side. Well over a hundred thousand weavers work at sixty thousand looms to turn out four-fifths of the country's commercial and export production. Here, as in most parts of India, it is the men who weave — very rarely, if at all, does the traditional pile carpet come from the hands of a woman.

Carpets are said to have been made here since the 16th century, the skills brought by Persian weavers during the reign of Emperor Akbar. There is another and rather romantic story of how weaving began; a Persian artisan was on the road, so the legend goes, when his caravan was attacked by brigands who robbed and massacred the travellers. Only the Persian escaped with his life and was made welcome by the villagers of Bhadohi, where he settled. As thanksgiving for their kindness he taught them the art of carpet knotting, which has flourished here since that time. True or not, the story has persisted as part of local history.

Sultanabad, Mirzapur-Bhadohi, wool, 245 knots per sq.in. In the detail shown here, giant palmettes are woven on a field of black.

opp. Bakhtiari, Mirzapur-Bhadohi, wool, 320 knots per sq.in. The panels of this elegant carpet have different yet subtle ground colours, each filled with flowers emerging from vases, a traditional Indo-Persian theme.

Mirzapur, once the greatest trading centre in northern India, declined when the railway to Allahabad was opened in 1864. By this time the carpet industry had taken firm root there, for it is recorded that carpets from Mirzapur were exhibited in Paris at the Exposition of 1867 and won much acclaim there.

In this predominantly rural setting, where it is not uncommon to see carpets travelling to factories in bullock carts or on bicycles wheeled through mustard fields, the marriage of traditional skills and modern technology is a sound management tool. And this has been used effectively by Obeetee, the largest manufacturer of hand-knotted and hand-tufted

carpets in the area. Their production is oriented to the export market, where swiftly changing demands are the real determinant for design and material. Though the colour plate for the design is still painstakingly created by a master artist or painted on graph paper, one knot per square, the use of computers speeds up subsequent processes. The computers store the master design, each pixel representing one knot, and a click of the mouse can change colours and shapes, or add and delete elements of patterning, allowing for design flexibility and cutting down response times to buyers from days to mere seconds. Designs can be executed directly on the computer, too, and a young generation of artists confidently uses the screen to express their inherited skills.

In the Mirzapur-Bhadohi area, many Persian designs are still used, such as the Qum (here called Ghoum). Traditional designs known to be local to this area include those named Rajasthan and Sirdar with plain fields and muted colours, their borders of soft rose, honey and green. Reproductions of Aubusson and Savonnerie patterns were given local names, such as Kandhari and Kalabar and made in the pastels favoured by Europeans.

Ghoum (Qum), Mirzapur-Bhadohi, wool, 414 knots per sq.in.
This traditional Indo-Persian design with its characteristic panels is here very finely executed, the effect enhanced by the use of soft, warm colours.

Over the years, the Mirzapur-Bhadohi belt acquired a reputation of mass producing for a mass market. It is true that the standard of weaving can vary substantially; equally, it is unfair to dismiss all its carpets as being coarse of structure. The finest type, which involves three or four highly-skilled artisans labouring shoulder to shoulder for months on the loom, can go to over four hundred knots per square inch.

The production of hand-tufted carpets has increased greatly, and this is one occupation where women as well as men work. In this process, the pile (or more accurately, tuft) is created by inserting lengths of wool on the foundation — on which the design has been transferred — by means of a tufting gun. When the whole area has been covered, the woollen tufts are secured with a coat of latex applied to the back of the carpet. A carpet can be made ready in a fraction of the time it takes for the hand-knotted type, which leads to the inevitable repercussion on price; both are handmade, no doubt, but the levels of skill and finesse are quite different. Technology has greatly improved the look and quality of hand-tufted carpets, so much so that the coarser hand-knotted carpets face real competition from those that have been tufted and, some feel, may even be in danger of dying out.

KASHMIR

If the Mirzapur-Bhadohi belt has the largest production in India, then indisputably Kashmir has its finest. Part of the refinement may stem from the fact that many carpet weavers came from the shawl industry, bringing with them the exquisite grace of execution that was such a hallmark of Kashmiri shawls. There is magic in the hands of the Valley craftsmen, they

say, and that magic seems to have persisted through all the ups and downs of the history of the carpet in this area.

The original carpets of Kashmir are said to be the gift of its far-sighted ruler, Zain-ul-Abidin. This early 15th century king had spent some years as a youth in Samarqand, held hostage there by Timur; in that dazzling court, Timur had gathered some of the finest

Modi Kashan, Kashmir, single-knotted, silk on silk, 484 knots per sq.in. The field of this beautiful carpet seems to shimmer in the light. The detailing of trees and flowering plants within the arch or mihrab is exquisite, as is the elaborate border.

Shawl carpet, Kashmir, single-knotted, wool, 231 knots per sq.in. So called because the paisley was a favourite motif of Kashmiri shawls.

craftsmen from the countries under his sway. When the young prince returned, he invited some of them to return with him. Some he sent for, from Persia and Central Asia, among them the weavers of hand-knotted carpets who set about training the local craftsmen. To Zain-ul-Abidin goes the credit of establishing the first karkhanas or factories where weaving, clipping and washing carpets were undertaken in an almost assembly line fashion. After his death, the industry seems to have gone into a decline until its revival during Mughal times.

In 1580 Akbar brought Kashmir into his empire; during his era, however, it was the shawl whose development was prominent. It was not until the reign of his son, Jehangir, that the revival of carpets took place, thanks to an energetic scholar named Akhun Rahnuma who, while returning from a pilgrimage to Mecca, acquired both the techniques and the tools from Persia. In this revival Akhun

Rahnuma was greatly helped by the Governor, Ahmed Beg Khan; and, of course, the patronage of the Emperor, whose eye for beauty was equalled by his love for Kashmir. After the Mughals, carpets retreated into the background once again as shawls took centre stage. This was the era of massive exports of shawls, a source of tremendous revenue to Kashmir's rulers. In the 19th century, during the Dogra period, the export market for shawls collapsed, throwing hundreds of weavers out of work; many of them turned their hand to carpets, whose next revival took place around that time. Because of the skills developed by shawls, they were able to accomplish the most minute knotting, a characteristic of Kashmir carpets to this day. Western interest was stimulated by the Great Exhibition of 1851, where a silk-warped pile carpet with seven hundred knots per square inch was displayed, and it was not long before systematic manufacture, mainly for export, began.

It is in the method of weaving — or, more properly, knotting — that the fine hand of the craftsman is apparent. Whereas in other parts the knot is tied around two warp threads, here it is tied around just one, leading to a higher density of knots to the square inch, and consequently a great depth and clarity of design. Another difference is in the method of "reading" the design; the role of the naksha placed on the loom or by its side is here taken by the talim, an adaptation from the weaving of shawls. This is a roll of paper marked with a code, which looks rather like a series of hieroglyphs, to indicate the number of knots to be woven in their respective colours. Each colour, for example anari (pomegranate red), zard (yellow), gulabi (pink), has a different sign. The master-weaver chants aloud from it, and the knotters follow his directions carefully, singing out their confirmation that the colours have been knotted.

The preparation of the talim calls for painstaking effort, and the job of a talim writer demands skill and experience. Strips of paper are made to translate the design and colours, each strip with twenty five squares representing one knot each. Imagine how many strips have to be made for a high knottage carpet! At least eight hundred strips are needed for a carpet with an all-over design, a task that could well take months.

We have seen that during Jehangir's time fine pashmina wool was knotted into pile carpets, and we may assume that the wool came from Kashmir, whose artisans were masters in the cleaning, spinning and dyeing of this fragile material. Once famous for its woollen carpets, today it is silk that dominates, and the highest quality use silk as warp

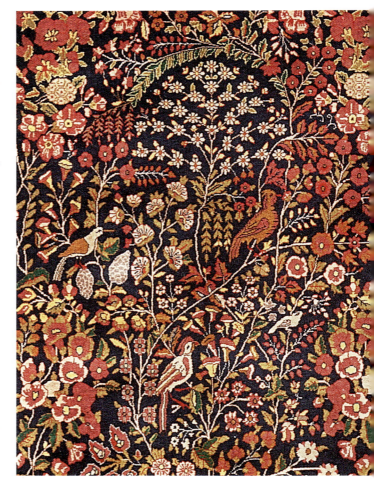

and weft as well as pile. The lustre of the silk gives a multi-hued appearance to the ground colour, which seems to change with every shift of light creating the effect of infinite reflections. A fibre whose use has been steadily on the increase is staple rayon silk, decried by purists since it is synthetic and should have no place in a product of such high artistry. It is true that it makes the carpet more affordable; equally, there is the danger that the artificial fibre is often passed off as the real thing to the unwary buyer.

There is an interesting mix of designs in the Kashmiri repertoire; the overwhelming influence of Persia, of course, in motifs and styling; but also distinctly Central Asian and Caucasian themes, as for example the Saroukh Turkoman (pg 18) and the Ardebil (pg 80). Central Asian medallions and hunting and polo scenes were part of the traditional patterns. Mughal

Three Bird Kirman, Kashmir, single-knotted, wool, 240 knots per sq.in. The richly-detailed carpet (see opp.) uses warm colours for the design; note the tone-on-tone, used to good effect on borders and field.

carpets have also been a source of inspiration, their flowering plants and chrysanthemum blooms reproduced in fine detail. Whatever the source, the Kashmiri designer added his own touch to each, drawing from the abundance of natural beauty around him to depict trees and flowers such as the rose, the crocus and the water lily. The colours are often subdued and muted, a range of taupes, eau-de-nils and pale blues; and sometimes rich and vibrant, standing out in bold relief against deep grounds. When vegetable colours were used, the purest yellow came from the saffron crocus flower, grown around the area of Pampore.

Kirman Laver Rahadaar, Kashmir, single-knotted, wool on wool, 431 knots per sq.in. Close-up of the field on pg 34.

The pile carpet, however, is not the only floor covering that Kashmir is famous for. Indigenous to the region is the gabba, called the "poor man's carpet", made of used blankets which are washed, milled and dyed. The pieces are then stitched together on a backing of cotton cloth, and can be embroidered or appliqued or both in bright colours that give it a rustic flavour. The best known, however, are numdahs and hook rugs, also called chain stitch rugs. Numdahs are pressed felt, usually made of wool, and embroidered in chain stitch with woollen yarn. Most of the designs feature florals, and many the delicate beauty of the chinar leaf. The hook rug is made on thick jute and covered completely with chain stitch so that the ground does not show. It gets its name from the hooked awl, or ari, used to execute the stitches; it is of comparatively recent origin and was once extremely popular as a floor covering.

Detail of a hook rug in chain stitch, Kashmir. The ground is made interesting with a pattern of whorls; the floral motif and colours are typical.

JAIPUR

Jaipur has been connected to carpets for the better part of four centuries, featuring both as a production centre and certainly as a lavish patron. The old capital of the Kachhwaha clan, rulers of Jaipur, was the fortress palace of Amer strategically situated on a rocky bluff eleven kilometres outside the present city. From its high walls and honey-coloured ramparts they ruled for seven centuries, building the fortress anew and tightening their grip through military prowess and advantageous alliances, especially with the Mughals. Raja Man Singh was Akbar's military commander in the late 16th century, and he is attributed with the start of a vast carpet collection recognised as one of the world's finest, some parts of which can still be seen in two museums of Jaipur.

There are stories about the genesis of the collection. One story says that the earliest carpets were brought back from Herat in Afghanistan as part of war booty; what is more, it is claimed that the Raja summoned weavers from there to set up looms in his city and train local craftsmen. Whereas the first part of this tale may be fanciful, the second could have a germ of truth, for it is recorded that there was indeed a workshop in Amer for silk and woollen carpets before 1640. Another legend has it that the carpets were

Kassan, Jaipur, wool and cotton, 140 knots per sq.in. Detail from the corner of a richly-ornamented ivory carpet.

opp. Kassan, Jaipur, wool and cotton, 140 knots per sq.in. This classic Jaipur design features graceful arches that loop around the florals.

presented to the Raja by Shah Jehan in return for the land on which the Taj Mahal now stands. This is less likely, for in the collection there are many carpets whose shapes indicate that they were crafted for use in specific areas, probably within the palace at Amer.

In the 18th century, Maharaja Sawai Jai Singh shifted his capital to Jaipur, the first planned city in Northern India; but the collection of carpets, numbering over two hundred and sixty, remained in Amer, and it was not until the later part of the 19th century that it was brought to Jaipur. From the original inventory, we can gather that some were purchased or obtained in the reigns of Shah Jehan and Aurangzeb, many of these from the Imperial workshop in Lahore. In the collection are carpets which bear the distinct and unmistakable Mughal stamp in their rows of flowering plants and their rich red ground. And there are the grand Durbar carpets meant for the court, of which the Garden Carpet — seen in the first part of this book — was probably an example.

All of this tells us that the Rajas of Jaipur shared the Mughal taste for carpets, but what of their own workshop? There is a design named Jaipur Mughal, could it have originated from the royal karkhana? We do not know; there seems to be a curious gap between the 17th and

the 19th centuries when, as we shall see later, carpet weaving was introduced as an occupation for prisoners in jail, where the production included flat-weave durries as well as woollen pile carpets. Thus in Jaipur, as in Kashmir, the art of the carpet seems to have gone through ups and downs; but it is highly possible that there lingered a few small units; after all, there must have been somebody to teach the prisoners.

The raw material in terms of wool was always close at hand. In the arid northern and western parts of Rajasthan, livestock has traditionally formed the major means of sustenance for rural people

Circular carpet with flower pattern, Mughal, woven in Kashmir or Lahore, ca. 1650. From the Jaipur collection once held at Amer.

opp. Detail of border in a rich saffron colour; vegetable dyes were used for this carpet, seen in full on pg 52.

and today the state produces around 40% of the country's raw wool. The carpet industry, largely concentrated in the areas around Jaipur, is the biggest consumer of this wool, absorbing 85% of the output. Wool and its ancillaries, such as carding and spinning, and the clipping and washing of finished goods, provides employment to a large number of people.

This, together with the inherent Rajasthani talent for all manner of textiles, their exuberant use of colour and eye for design, may have influenced the entrepreneurs who chose to

Kassan, Jaipur, wool and cotton, 196 knots per sq.in. The blue-grey field is patterned with cream and beige palmettes.

establish the carpet industry in Jaipur. A census report reveals that in the 19th century more and more companies began to engage in this business, one of whom produced carpets of high quality with between one and four hundred knots per square inch. From the 1920s to the 1940s there was a mushroom growth of carpet producing companies. Business boomed because of the heavy demand in Western countries for oriental carpets; soon there were as many as fifty factories making carpets in Jaipur; but lack of quality control (speculators had by now entered the market for quick money) led to a serious crisis, and by the latter half of

Dholaraoji, Rajasthan, a typical village homestead with a loom shed, which has four looms for pile carpets.

below: Clipping a pile carpet to bring out its design; the clipped part is in the foreground.

the 1940s unsold stocks piled up in cities like London and Paris. Many factories had to shut down; in the early 1960s there were only four or five left.

It was a bitter lesson and it was learnt the hard way. But a bare twenty years later there was a resurgence of the carpet industry; today, thousands of artisans clustered around Jaipur earn their money from it; and although in terms of quantity the production is far smaller than that of Mirzapur-Bhadohi, its overall quality is considered higher.

The traditional designs of Jaipur carpets followed the general Indo-Persian trend. The grounds were deep, rich red, blue and ivory, the field shared by cypress trees and animals; there were floral carpets,

Kassan, Jaipur, wool and cotton, 140 knots per sq.in. The deep red field is a traditional colour, as are the design motifs such as the palmette.

of course, their borders traced with elaborate vines scrolled around blooms and buds. There were also the Indo-Herati designs, with small angular motifs enclosing little rosettes. Indo-Kirmans with ivory or cream fields were ornamented all over with sprays of flowers. Of late, the skills of vegetable dyes have been revived leading to warm, soft earth colours.

THE INDO-TIBETAN TRADITION

Someone once wrote that the carpet was "…the emblem of eternity and (its) pattern the visible world of change". Of no carpets can this be more true than those of the Indo-Tibetan tradition where the designs follow a symbology deeply rooted in faith. This carpet tradition originated in Tibet, as the name suggests, and extends across the Himalayan Buddhist belt stretching from Ladakh in the west to Sikkim and Arunachal Pradesh in the east. In addition there are a number of centres across the country where Tibetan refugees pursue this craft. Each area may have its own interpretations and distinct styles, but the basic tradition remains the same, shaped by the beliefs of the Vajrayana Buddhism of Tibet.

There are references to pile carpets in the biography of the great saint Milarepa (11th-12th centuries). As the credos of Vajrayana radiated outward from the high plateaux, the weaving of carpets spread to areas that came under its influence. There was a practical reason for this. In those cold climates carpets made of wool created an ambience of warmth, but very rarely were they made to use on the floor simply to tread on. They were woven for monasteries for daily or ritual use, for pack animals as saddle blankets, for households as sleeping or seating rugs, as cushion or pillow covers or meditation rugs, as door or pillar hangings. That is why many antique rugs are small, about three feet by six feet in size, to

cover the raised platforms that serve as both seating areas and beds in many Tibetan houses. It is only when commercial production started that the carpets were made larger for use as flooring. This wide variety of uses inherent in the culture forced, as it were, the decentralisation of their manufacture as that culture spread.

These functional objects were beautified and made meaningful with the use of colour and symbol. The designs reflect many influences, among them ancient pre-Buddhist culture and the iconography of Indian and Chinese Buddhism, manifesting in motifs such as the lotus, the vajra and the endless knot. The Chinese influence is especially clear in the fantasy shapes of the dragon and phoenix, the curled clouds and the small medallions characteristic of Chinese carpets. Stylised birds and flowers like the chrysanthemum were often woven. Local influences showed themselves in representations of the mythical snow lion, called cha in Ladakh and sengge in Sikkim.

Tibetan, wool. Three coins carpet; the coin is a secular symbol of prosperity and three is an auspicious number. The border has the endless knot, signifying the endless compassion of Buddha as well as earthly continuity.

A favourite theme is that of the Eight Auspicious Symbols. Each symbol has a meaning; for example, the umbrella is the ancient Indian symbol of protection and royalty, the lotus signifies purity and divinity, the endless knot is both the Buddha's infinite compassion as well as a secular symbol of continuity, the conch shell represents the deep and melodious resonance of Dharma teachings and the Dharma Chakra, the wheel of Buddha's doctrine. But here, as elsewhere, the designs of the carpets have changed with the demands of an overseas market.

The method of weaving in the Indo-Tibetan tradition is a little different from that in other areas. Here, a weaving rod is used to knot in the yarn; most carpets are knotted to densities of sixty, eighty or hundred knots per square inch. The finishing includes the "relief" cutting

of the pile to give it the characteristic three-dimensional look where areas stand out against the ground. Although both men and women work on the carpets, this is probably the tradition where women weavers outnumber men.

In these traditions from different parts of the country, we can see how a wide dispersal of carpet locations makes for a very rich variety. It is true that the overwhelming influences are common to all and easily traceable, but within those conventions the Indian artist and weaver added something new from his own experience that enriched the fabric and gave its design a different dimension. The adaptation of motifs, the balance of ornamentation came easily to the Indian hand, trained for centuries in the crafting of world-famous textiles. Carpets are amongst the finest examples of the "harmonious bloom of Indian textures" that was seen wherever there was a loom and a weaver.

Tibetan, wool. The central medallion is a four-headed vajra or dorji, quintessential symbol of Vajrayana Buddhism, as indestructible and brilliant as a diamond. The dorji forms the sceptre of peaceful divinities and the thunderbolt-like weapon of wrathful deities.

opp. Tibetan, wool. The central medallion represents a coin. On either side, there is a lotus, symbol of purity, divinity, compassion and renunciation.

f o u r

OF DURRIES AND PRISONS

In the palmy days of the Delhi Sultanate there existed a court functionary called the Mehtar Farrash, so a 13th century account tells us. His job description was that of carpet spreader, in which task he was assisted by numerous others.

From this, we may reasonably assume that there must have been a large number of carpets which needed to be spread: indeed, there was a whole department, the Farrashkhana, dedicated to the buying, storage and maintenance of such things as carpets, tents and canopies, a practice that continued into Mughal times. Battles and wars were lumbering affairs, entailing armies on the move for

opp. Cotton durrie from Palanpur in Gujarat, at least eighty years old. Vegetable dyes have been used on hand-spun yarn; on the border, a vine trails leaves and flowers in a graceful pattern.

months, hence the need for vast encampments and spreads for the ground. In courts and mosques, large halls had floor coverings of some sort for people to sit on; not surprising, then, that a special official was designated as the carpet overseer.

But what kind of carpets were these? The word given in the account, galim, is a bit confusing, since other accounts use it to mean pile carpets. Some interpret it as deriving from the Turkish kilim, whose modern meaning is a flat-woven carpet, the sort that in India is called durrie or shatrinji.

In all likelihood, a number of the carpets over which the Mehtar Farrash held charge must have been flat-woven, for such weaving was then prevalent in India, even as far south as Karnataka. And certainly they were made in the era of Akbar (16th century); the chronicler of that time, Abul Fazl, makes the all-important distinction between galims and shatrinjis in the Ain-i-Akbari, writing "The galims of Iran and Turan are no more thought of…It would take up too much time to describe the jajams, shatrinjis…and the fine mats which look as if woven of silk."

Corridor in Samode Palace Hotel, Rajasthan, its jewelled beauty enhanced by a succession of pastel durries

opp. A Sikh Noble, Pahari painting, first quarter of 19th c. A Sikh chieftain and his lady love share a glass of wine within a tent. Note the striped durrie underneath, on top of which is placed a floral carpet.

Dressing the warp with a drum, Banskho, near Jaipur. The length indicates that perhaps more than one durrie will be woven off this warp.

Traditionally, flat-woven carpets made by hand encompassed a wide spectrum of weavers and uses. At the village level, people wove them for their own use or to trade locally. In organised workshops, the production was commercial and often commissioned and hence

made to the specifications of the buyer. At one time, there were many centres for commercial durrie production, in districts like Warangal in Andhra Pradesh, Dharwar in Karnataka, Coimbatore in Tamil Nadu and Sirmaur in Himachal Pradesh, to name but a few.

Durries, which could be woven of wool or cotton but usually the latter, were not only ubiquitous but also versatile. They were spread on jute-strung cots, an underlay for the sheets and pillows used as bedding, a wrap for the bedding or bistra to be bundled into and stored away for the day. It was for just this purpose that young maidens in parts of Punjab, Haryana and Rajasthan wove durries in bright colours to carry as dowry or bridal rugs when they got married. Coarser varieties were placed on the floor for visitors, or used as sacking and cart covers. Small sizes were used as prayer mats, as asans by Hindus, most importantly in Islam, where the faithful followed the injunction of the five daily prayers (namaz), by kneeling on the sanctified space provided by these portable mats. Often the Islamic mats were woven with sacred symbols, the mihrab, for instance, the niche whose arch was always pointed towards Mecca while praying. Or a suspended lamp, perhaps meant to signify the infinite radiance of Allah as the source of all enlightenment. Domes and minarets of mosques were decorative and symbolic images woven on the mats. Not all prayer mats were made for

Durrie weaver on vertical loom, Banskho, near Jaipur, with the sample or naksha in the foreground.

Cotton durrie being woven on a horizontal loom in Rajasthan, where weavers are tamping the weft down with their comb-like panjas.

opp. Jail durrie sample; half of a jainamaz or Muslim prayer rug, with the domes and minarets of a mosque.

individual worship. In mosques, long narrow durries served as a sort of community prayer mat for a row of people, where individual spaces were marked out by repetitions of a symbol such as the mihrab; these were known as saphs.

The largest durries, however, were made for courtly and festive occasions. In the palaces of former times, halls of public audience were carpeted with durries, and palace durries are known to be as huge as twenty five feet by eighty feet: surely the largest hand made floor coverings in the world! Such large durries would have required specially sized looms and therefore were only made to order. It was not only in halls that royal durries were placed. They were also used in the tented camps set up during the many shikar or hunting expeditions of the Maharajas. Today in India we know the durrie as a staple floor or ground covering for any occasion where groups of people congregate, and no caterer or tent supplier worth the name can afford to be without durries in different sizes.

For many of us, the most familiar durrie designs are those of basic stripes — usually the red and blue so beloved of caterers — lozenges and squares. Sir George Birdwood, writing in the early 20th century on the industrial arts of India (for such was the quaint name given to money-earning crafts), rhapsodised that these " …illustrate the most ancient ornamental designs in India, perhaps earlier even than the migration of the Aryas." This theory may be more romantic than factual; nonetheless, miniature paintings dating from the 16th century onwards show the use of striped durries in court, usually in blue and white, sometimes with carpets laid on top of them. By the end of the 17th century, paintings from different regions of India featured the durrie, confirming their widespread use throughout the country.

The patronage of royal or wealthy clients maintained the art of the durrie, and many fine examples were woven in former states such as Baroda and Jaisalmer, amongst others. But in the 19th and early 20th centuries certain developments gave it an impetus. The first was the Crystal Palace Exhibition in London in 1851,

which drew the attention of European merchants to Indian carpets; pile carpets, admittedly, but the growing interest in Indian floor coverings was sharpened by another exhibition, this time in Delhi in 1902, which had a special section on durries. Between the two exhibitions, while implementing jail reforms the visionary Maharaja of Jaipur, Sawai Ram Singh II, was one of the first to introduce the weaving of durries in jail. The objectives were laudable. Not only did it give prisoners a creative occupation and infuse new life into the craft, the sale of these contributed money towards administrative and other costs of the jail. The Maharaja's initiative was copied by other jails, including those in British India; by the beginning of the 20th century, prisons all over the country were weaving durries, many even the pile carpet. A story goes that the Maharaja of Bikaner, on a visit to England, asked his manager to buy him a choice carpet, only to find, when the costliest available was unrolled in front of

Jail durrie sample. This narrow strip, of which we can see the front and back, is technically accomplished as we can see from the fine workmanship.

below: Jail durrie sample. This brightly coloured one-quarter sample features a red-and-green Chamba design with five stems representing the five elements

opp.right: Jail durrie sample. Against the deep red ground are shown treatments and colours possible in florals and borders.

opp.left: Jail durrie sample. Typically, this has different floral motifs and ground colours for weavers to copy.

him, that it had been woven in one of his own jails! Some of the most beautiful durries were crafted during this time in the prisons of Bikaner, Poona, Agra, Lucknow and of course Jaipur; other centres in the former undivided India included Lahore and Multan. The new patrons were the officials of the Raj who used durries lavishly in both their homes and Government offices.

Training prisoners was no easy task, and the individual had to progress through stages marked by different kinds of patterns, starting with simple stripes and on to more complicated geometrics before graduating to the ultimate refinement of the

pictorial durrie. This last called for a highly skilful hand to execute curvilinear patterns. The weaving process began with the stretched warp whose tension had to be high and constant for the even edges and symmetry demanded by the form. The weft yarn was used like a shuttle; bound into different coloured bundles, it was inserted, colour by colour, through the warp threads to the width required by the design, then turned around the next warp. Where two weft yarns of different colours met in the same line, they were dovetailed, that is, both were turned around the same warp, one above the other. Thus the weaver progressed line by line, tamping down the lines of the weft with an implement, like the panja (a comb-like tool) in Rajasthan. The durries were called "weft-faced", meaning that the visible surface is all weft, the warp being hidden underneath. Today's weavers use the same technique, working off looms that can be horizontal or vertical with warps stretched by hand or tautened on large drums.

Jail durrie sample, probably an asan or Hindu prayer mat. The colours and stepped pyramid motifs are typical.

opp. Corner of an alcove, Samode Palace Hotel, Rajasthan. The durrie-on-durrie creates a harmony of colours with the painted walls.

As the production in prisons increased, so did the variety of designs, and small samples were made as references from which larger durries could be replicated. The designs came from older durries, or were adapted from pile carpets, or taken from books. To this day, some of the older jails have their own small collection of sample durries from the hey-day of prison weaving, of poignant interest to the viewer as much for the designs and colours (many now forgotten) as for the circumstances in which they were created.

For many reasons, the durrie went into a kind of decline after being in vogue in the early decades of the 20th century, and for years the commercial output was largely pedestrian, the colours and designs repetitive, the status relegated to a cheap and utilitarian covering of no great distinction. It took almost five decades for the durrie to go through the brilliant renaissance that brought it back on the Indian and then world scene.

This re-birth was precipitated by the coming together of circumstances and individuals. After the Partition of India, skilled durrie weavers were amongst the migrants who were resettled in areas in and around Panipat in Haryana. But the competition from the faster, cheaper output of mills was intense, so they had to turn to a different style of presentation in order to make a mark. Old designs of florals and geometrical motifs were revived, and the colour palette revitalised from harsh aniline dyes to softer Indian colours. Outlets such as Fabindia and the Cottage Industries Emporium, both from nearby Delhi, were amongst the first to retail these durries.

But say durrie, and one name comes to mind — that of Shyam Ahuja, to whom goes the credit of placing the durrie firmly on the international

Cotton durrie, Jaipur. The plain field is set off by the contrasting colour of the border and its design.

opp. Cotton durrie runner, Jaipur. The flowering plants are taken from old Mughal carpet designs.

market. His first durrie was a result of pure chance; while trying to sell carpets overseas, he received an order for a cotton flat-weave durrie. The execution was so successful that more were commissioned. From this beginning came the whole range that made him famous, the soft pastel colours, the designs adapted from architectural forms, from sari motifs: in short, a look and feel far removed from the traditional concepts of the durrie. Durries soon became the rage and entire villages in U.P. and Rajasthan turned to the craft as

Cotton durrie, Jaipur. The theme of the flowering plant that dominates the deep blue field is subtly and elegantly echoed in the ivory border.

other exporters entered the market. While the men did the weaving, the women washed them to give the required finish. Soon, silk and wool durries were being made in addition to those of cotton; from an ordinary floor covering, the durrie vaulted into the high life, becoming what one exporter calls " a life-style product, a fashion product". Exports were spurred by the imaginative use of colours in changing combinations, and fresh

Tie-dye cotton yarn ready for durrie weaving in Rajasthan.

designs and textures. That was a time when more durries were exported from India than any other floor covering from any other part of the world.

The export market has since peaked, and though the overseas demand continues, much of its initial hunger has been satiated. The weaving of durries today is sustained by an increasing interest from the domestic market, for whom this versatile floor covering is affordable, contemporary and well-suited to local climates.

f i v e

Preserving the Heritage

$\mathcal{S}$o far we have looked at a selection of pile carpets and durries from specific locations, but that is not the whole story. Within the overall ambit of handmade floor coverings there are many other forms, such as gabbehs, numdahs, druggets, kilims, soumaks and rugs. The materials used go beyond wool, silk and cotton to embrace varieties of synthetic fibres; the designs and colours may not be easily recognisable as "Indian" or even "Indo-Persian" because the production is geared to demand and includes abstract patterning and contemporary themes selected by buyers. Nor are the production areas confined to the ones mentioned in earlier chapters; the spread is wide, and features places like Amritsar, Agra, Panipat, Bikaner,

opp. Ardebil, Kashmir, single-knotted, wool, 256 knots per sq.in. A traditional Caucasian design, whose bold lines and sweeping patterning look almost contemporary.

A richly-patterned ivory carpet from Jaipur. Such hand-knotted carpets now face competition from those that are machine made.

Gwalior, Danapur, and Elluru and Warangal in Andhra Pradesh, to name just some important centres. We have dwelt on aspects of history and craft for a better understanding of the meaning of carpets; behind this lies the business of carpets and the questions that now confront the people in that business.

Across the country over twenty five lakh people (two and a half million) earn their daily bread from the manufacture of handmade floor coverings, whether they are loom owners or weavers, suppliers or people involved in separate parts of the process such as dyers or finishers. The largest part of what they produce goes for export; it is not surprising, then, that producers are sensitive to the international market, the backbone of their business. The major handmade carpet producing countries include Iran, China, Pakistan and Turkey; India's share of the world market is around 17% and her biggest buyers are the United States and Europe, where Germany leads.

But marketplaces are notoriously volatile areas, competitive, challenging, with sudden variables that can upset equations built painstakingly over decades of trade. Yet there are opportunities, too, for those who seize the moment. The Indian carpet industry stands at precisely such a cross-roads, and because of the social, economic and heritage implications, a view of the current situation is also a view of the issues that face it.

Part of the challenge lies in the perception and meaning of the carpet itself. Fine quality hand-knotted carpets woven on the loom are at the high end of the spectrum and priced to match; they were once regarded as an investment for life, and valued for their beauty and artistry. Today, like much else, carpets have become a "fashion" or "life-style" acquisition,

trendy rather than timeless. So the long
months taken on the loom to create a
work of art may be too long for those
looking for a faster turnover. Some of
the most classic designs, the sort at
which the Indian weavers excel, are too
conservative, too formal, for
contemporary taste, but there is no
significant stock of locally-developed
designs to augment or replace them. A
big body-blow was delivered by the
controversial question of child labour on
the looms, a complex and vexing issue.
Add to that the growing competition
from countries like China and Iran, the
general slowdown in world economy,
the conversion from a seller's market to
one where the buyer dominates, and
one can see why growth has dropped
from the boom of the 1970s and 1980s
to a meagre figure (around 3%) today.
Within that growth the ratios of what is

being made have changed, with a fall-off in hand-knotted carpets, itself a cause of alarm for preservers of heritage.

The bulk of our carpets are not made in factories but are part of a cottage industry. The scale here is human and so are the problems; child labour is one of them, especially in the Mirzapur-Bhadohi area and further east into Bihar. Overseas buyers under pressure from concerned consumer groups and

Seating area, Samode Palace Hotel, Rajasthan: a symphony of blues where a finely-knotted pile carpet is placed on a durrie, a tradition often seen in miniature paintings.

human rights watchers threatened a boycott of Indian goods unless steps were taken to remedy the situation. Quite rightly so — it can be nobody's case that this practice continue; but there is more than one side to this question, and many grey areas. This is a desperately poor part of India and sometimes a child's earnings are a matter of bread for the whole family. Further, this is a skill that has to be acquired young: like every art its transmission depends on early training: what, then, will happen in the future? Already, some in the industry foresee a time when the finest knotting will no longer be possible because there will be few weavers left at that level of artistry.

Close up of traditional palmette motif from a Jaipur carpet.

opp. Children in Mirzapur-Bhadohi, where child labour is an issue. Some are in school uniform; the sign on the door states that no one below the age of fourteen works here.

Surely the long term answer must lie in a humane and compassionate approach that recognises the reality of the milieu while tackling the problem. Several such initiatives have been taken, involving the cooperation of exporters, loom owners, activists and the Government. The Carpet Export Promotion Council, set up by the Government, instituted the Kaleen label for just this purpose. Under Indian law, anyone below fourteen years of age qualifies as a child and is prohibited from employment. Exemptions are granted to children working in their family home where specialised crafts are passed from one generation to the next; however, the concern is for those children who work outside their domestic environment, and often far away from it. Carpets stamped with the Kaleen label represent the industry's commitment to the

eradication of such child labour, the welfare and medical care of the weaver community, the education and rehabilitation of children and their vocational training with a stipend. The last is a practical means of replacing the much-needed wages of children taken out of the labour pool.

Looms and exporters must be registered with the Council, such registration being mandatory to engage in export. Council members have to follow the Child Labour Code of Conduct, which commits that no children work on the looms, which are subject to surprise checks by an independent body as part of the monitoring system. Violators can be punished by having their export privileges cancelled. In addition, large private companies such as Obeetee in Mirzapur organised awareness

campaigns against illegal child labour, got
written assurances from loom owners, and
instituted their own inspection system to ensure
compliance in the four thousand-odd looms
where their work is executed. Since 1995,
Council members have contributed part of their
export earnings to a welfare fund dedicated to
the establishment of schools with mid-day
meals, among other benefits.

Child labour, however, is only one aspect of the
larger social scenario that concerns the mega
buyers, the really big names from overseas who
order in bulk. Now aesthetics must go hand in
hand with social accountability, a term which
includes examining the conditions under which
all work is done and making sure that labour

Hemp durrie, Rajasthan. One of the new materials being used
for floor coverings.

opp. Jute durrie, Rajasthan, an innovative texture in a product
developed by an exporter in Jaipur. Subtly striped, its traditional
weave is executed in the desert areas of Barmer.

laws are followed. Looms and premises must be open to inspection so that stringent social audits can be carried out; if this sounds presumptuous of the buyer, it must be remembered that large companies are very sensitive to media and public opinion in their home countries. Buyers and wholesalers must answer to retailers and, eventually, the consumer. A boycott hurts everybody, most especially the weaver.

This difficult situation is compounded by dwindling demand and depressed prices. Set in the context of increasing competition from other countries, it has meant an excess of supply. Fluctuations in tastes lead to feast or famine situations; silk carpets were all the rage a few years ago and exports shot up, but now have fallen off. Clearly there is need for revitalisation and new directions.

The industry has to re-invent itself, say people from within, and regain world-wide pre-eminence through a proactive approach to product development and design. This is the only key to survival. Other countries have faster turn-out times at lower prices, and if the battle cannot be joined on grounds of price, then the product must be superior. New colours, new textures, new designs — these are all critical to the process.

An example of a hand-tufted carpet. The production of these carpets is on the rise as they are extremely popular.

opp. Awaiting the loom: dyed yarn in a carpet factory.

The recent success story has been in hand-tufted carpets, whose popularity has grown in the last few years thanks to its low pricing and easy replaceability, very much part of the "use and throw" culture. Conversely, as the tufted quality has improved with technology, there has been a falling off in the production of coarser, less expensive hand-knotted carpets.

It is a delicate balancing act between the very real need to preserve inherited skills and the demands of the marketplace, calling for sensitive intervention. In the initiatives it has taken, the Carpet Export Promotion Council acts upon different aspects of the totality. One is the development of new markets, which may be small in themselves but could add up significantly, such as Latin America and South Asia. Regional areas are being examined as sources for the creation of a new, indigenous design vocabulary, places like Gujarat, the Deccan and the North East. At the same time, the evaluation of design requirement from buyer countries and keeping abreast with what is current, continues. Even more deep-rooted is the plea to Government for the reconsideration of labour laws.

In an industry which is so labour-intensive and where demand is so

unstable, existing labour laws are stringent enough to deter would-be entrepreneurs from setting up carpet factories. Yet there is need to bring the unorganised sector into the organised sector, into a factory environment where productivity can be improved, quality monitored, and an economy of scale achieved. This can only happen if labour laws are specially modified or created for the cottage sector which take into account its peculiarities while protecting the interests of the worker. China's more flexible labour laws, in fact, are quoted by industry people across the spectrum as a major reason for its success.

Around the globe, handmade carpets and floorings are facing intense competition from those made by machine. This, too, is of concern to the Council. In a bold move, it has called for the establishment of a World Forum which brings together under a single umbrella all the countries producing handmade carpets and floor coverings to promote and brand these products. Transcending national rivalries and coming together to propagate the inherent beauty and artistry of the hand-crafted object is a key part of the agenda.

In India, though, articles made by hand represent much more than beauty, or a skills heritage that can never be replicated mechanically. They are the livelihood of millions of workers who live in villages but are not farmers; whatever benefits they earn have a ripple effect which has an impact on the lives of further millions. It is as much for this reason as to keep alive the cherished heritage of excellence that the survival of the hand-knotted carpet industry is important to us all.

Taking a carpet to the factory, Mirzapur-Bhadohi.
Here, as elsewhere, the larger part of weaving is done in rural areas.

SELECT BIBLIOGRAPHY

Flowers Underfoot: Indian Carpets of the Mughal Era, Daniel Walker
Thames and Hudson, London, 1998

Indian Carpets, E. Gans-Ruedin
Thames and Hudson, London, 1984

Indian Carpets and Floor Coverings, Kamaladevi Chattopadhyay
All India Handicrafts Board, New Delhi, 1966

Dhurrie: Flatwoven Rugs of India, Shyam Ahuja, Meera Ahuja, Mridula Maluste,
India Book House, Mumbai, 1999

The Unappreciated Dhurrie, Steven Cohen, David Black & Clive Loveless (eds),
David Black Oriental Carpets, London, 1982

The Country Life Book of Rugs and Carpets of the World, Ian Bennett (ed),
Country Life Books, London, 1978

The Glory of Indian Handicrafts, Kamaladevi Chattopadhyay
Indian Book Co., 1976

Oriental Carpets, Giovanni Curatola
Souvenir Press, 1983

World Rugs and Carpets, David Black (ed)
Country Life Books, London, 1985

Industrial Arts of India, G. C. M. Birdwood
Rupa & Co., New Delhi, 1988

Census of India 1961, Rajasthan, Carpets of Jaipur, C. S. Gupta
Goverment of India, New Delhi, 1966

The Encyclopaedia of Tibetan Symbols and Motifs, Robert Beer
Serindia Publications, London

ACKNOWLEDGEMENTS & PICTURE CREDITS

For permisssion to photograph from their collections, and on locations, we would like to thank:

The Government Central Museum, Jaipur, pp 3, 6, 8-9, 11, 12, 13, 14, 16, 20, 21, 22, 26, 27, 29, 32, 33, 55, 56-57, 58; photographer Mahesh Hariani
Thanks to Mr. Pankaj Dharendra, Curator, for his assistance.

Obeetee Pvt. Ltd., Mirzapur and Bhadohi, pp 25 (both), 36, 37 (both), 39, 40, 41, 42-43, 87, 90, 92; photographer S. S. Rattan
Thanks to Mr. Edward Oakley, Chairman, and Mr. V. R. Sharma, Managing Director, for all their assistance.

Jaipur Central Jail, Jaipur, pp 71, 72 (both), 73 (both), 74; photographer Mahesh Hariani
Thanks to Mr. Balbhadra Singh, Director General, Rajasthan Police, for assistance.

Ambika Exports, Jaipur, pp 64, 76, 77, 78, 88; photographer Mahesh Hariani
Thanks to Mr. Brijendra Rajpal, Managing Partner, Ambika Exports for his assistance.

Jaipur Carpets, Jaipur, pp 5, 52, 53, 54, 56-57, 58 (both), 59, 68, 69, 70, 79, 82, 86, 89, 91; photographer Mahesh Hariani
Thanks to Mr. N. K. Choudhary for his assistance.

Gulam Mohidin and Son, New Delhi, pp 1, 2, 18, 24, 30-31, 34, 45, 46, 48, 49, 50, 51, 80; photographer Avinash Pasricha
Thanks to Ms. Sarvat Amin for her assistance.

Rani Saheba Arpana Kumari of Samode, pp 67, 75, 84-85; photographer Mahesh Hariani

For permission to use images from their collections, we would like to thank the following:

Bharat Kala Bhavan, Varanasi, "The Offended Mistress", page 19

The Directorate of Archaeology, Archives and Museums, Jammu and Kashmir Government
"The Abhisarika", page 28, from the Dogra Art Gallery, Jammu

Government Museum and Art Gallery, Chandigarh, "A Sikh Noble", page 66

H. H. The Dalai Lama's Charitable Trust Handicrafts Exports, New Delhi,
pages 61, 62, 63
Thanks to Mr. Tsultrim Dorjee, General Manager, for his assistance

Thanks also to
Mr. Vijay Thakur, Chairman of the Carpet Export Promotion Council and
Mr. Gaurav Sharma, Senior Vice-President, Obeetee,
both in New Delhi, for providing valuable inputs for the last chapter.

And special thanks to Pankaj and Kirti Madhok in Jaipur, without whom so much would not
have been possible.